CRACKING THE CODE

CRACKING THE CODE

DAVID BERGMAN

1985 GEORGE ELLISTON POETRY PRIZE

OHIO STATE UNIVERSITY PRESS □ COLUMBUS

Copyright © 1985 by the Ohio State University Press.
All Rights Reserved.

Library of Congress Cataloguing in Publication Data

Bergman, David, 1950–
  Cracking the code.

  I. Title.
PS3552.E71933C7   811'.54   85-15227
ISBN 0-8142-0394-9

FOR BOB HELSLEY

CONTENTS

ACKNOWLEDGMENTS

I would like to thank the following for permission to reprint poems that first appeared in their pages: *American Scholar*, for "Actors' Equity," "Aunt Ida's Last Evasion," "Old Man Sitting in a Shopping Mall," and "Rubenesque"; *Baltimore Jewish Times*, for "The Ballad of Aunt Rose"; *Christopher Street*, for "Exchanges" and "Blueberry Man"; *College English*, for "The Dancer Denies a Suitor"; *Kenyon Review*, for "Cardiogram," "The Dedicant," and "Elective Surgery"; *Michigan Quarterly Review*, for "Eclogue": *Mouth of the Dragon*, for "No Knowledge But as Recollection"; *Paris Review*, for "The Artist Is No Physician" and "The Miniaturist"; *Raritan*, for "Urban Renewal" and "Seduction at Camden Passage"; *Shenandoah*, for "In and Out of the Garden" and "The Laying On of Hands"; *South Carolina Review*, for "Intercepted Courier"; *Virginia Quarterly Review*, for "Doldrums"; and *Yale Review*, for "The Madame Considers Her Future State."

I would also like to express my appreciation for the help Daniel Mark Epstein, Donald Craver, and Richard Howard have given me, and Helen Jones for typing and retyping the manuscript. Part of the work on this collection was completed with the help of a summer research grant from Towson State University.

CRACKING THE CODE

ELECTIVE SURGERY

No accusations, love, about the past.
    Think only of the pleasures of this night,
all that we have made together. What false
    note could have lead to such a harmony
that silence resounds with the after-
    shock of love? Nothing is missing.
Nor have I tried to keep you in the dark,
    hid behind lies, avoided certain facts.
Yet since life is nothing but change, I thought
    before I told you how I came to be,
you first should know the woman that I am.
    What loss is there in that? Yet like the rest
of them, you also say I've squandered
    my treasures in a moment of frivolity.
Go on. No need to hide it. You wear
    the same sad look my surgeon wore the day
before the operation, when he came
    to ask if I really meant to have it done.
"The rest we can undo," he said,
    "but this is irreversible." How I wanted
to say, "Please, you're lifting a terrible burden
    from me. Let it be gone. Let it be done.
I have been pricked enough!" But doctors,
    my dear, they have no sense of humor. All
I could say was I was sure.
                    But I thought,
how strange, on this the day of my liberation
    he should ask if I really loved
my chains. Were others such servants of
    their masculinity, that like house slaves
after the Civil War, they would return
    to their masters and forget their freedom.

But then the orderly entered with his bowl
    of shaving lather and a razor

to prep me for the knife. A young boy
        barely out of school. His hand shook as he
brought the blade to my pubic hair.
        "I'm always afraid I'll nick somebody here,"
he told me. "Well, in my case, it all comes off
        in the morning. Hack away."
But that only made him shakier. In fact he did
        nick me. Right at the side. I bled and
thought—such crazy thoughts—that this is how
        a virgin bleeds, that this shy and
nervous lad was taking my innocence away!
        And I moaned so loud he must have thought
I was really hurt and rubbed me nearly raw
        with styptic pencil.
                                That night
I had a dream. No, not about dying,
        but about my unborn soul, my soul
before it knew its body. An angel
        was leading me through racks of flesh neatly
displayed on hangers like suits in a store.
        Already we had looked through fox and weasel
(too furry), whale and seal (the oil!),
        giraffe and armadillo. But no success:
before me stretched all manner of human shape,
        each color, height and weight, not simply
in fetal stages, but as child, adult and
        adolescent. I had narrowed it down
to a sultry secretary, platinum blond
        and quick as a stenographer's pencil,
and a petite brunette who burns away her life
        of quiet intensity in Tarrytown
or Rye. And just when I had made my decision,
        what should they bring through the double doors,
but a new line of junior executives.

They are committed to free will in Heaven.
        Satan, I'm sure, was never taken aside

by the Father and given The Word of
        advice, or made to lie on some golden couch
and urged to recall the birth of his
        insecurities. Besides, my angel
would have been no help, having spent
        his days on earth a bankrupt drunk in Bliss,
a small town in Tennessee. How unfair
        to have a spirit who's never seen
the other side of life make important
        choices on his own.
                                How could I know
that the beauty I desired in others
        was not the same I wanted for myself,
that what I found so noble and so strong
        on the faces of men would never fit me?
A child does not know this, and I was less
        than a child. He sees a bird and wants
wings of his own; he sees a fish and would
        swim breathless through the water.
I could not understand, pure spirit
        that I was, the sculptor does not wish
to turn to stone, the singer into song.
        If in my dream I chose to be a man, it was—
it is because in dreams all loving is alike.

Awake the differences are clear, my needs
        more urgent still. I should have taken life
as it came, you're thinking. Accepted it.
        But why of all the facts of life must sex
be the unalterable condition,
        the absolute given we are born to?
Were body only a clothing for the soul
        to keep it warm and hold it fast together,
any sex would do. We could wear the baggy
        pants of our fathers, the cast-off skins
of cobras, or like some crabs, the oversized shells
        of mollusks. We'd refuse tight-fitting

garments like frugal mothers who demand
    a year's use and room to grow in.

But haven't we discovered again tonight
    that body is much more than outerwear,
more than the exposed wire of our energy
    though it sparks and shocks and burns.
Love, put your arms once more around
    this twice-transforming flesh, and feel
all I ever should have been, all I ever need to be.

COMFORT

To be ill
is to be another person.
    —Denton Welch

The ill can best amuse each other
or so my mother thought. Why else
would I have spent each afternoon
playing bingo with Mrs. Bernstein
our neighbor going blind from diabetes?

Don't get him too excited, my mother warned,
afraid the clot that blocked my brain
like a cork in a bottle of pop, would burst
were I rattled too hard. Mrs. Bernstein
paid no attention. Instead she told me
tales of growing up in Warsaw, of feeding
caged geese outside the butcher's doorway,
of marching guards outside the palace gates,
of looking through the window of her father's
store at the beautiful fedoras, crisp bowlers
and handsome derbies he imported from Italy
and which he wore home, a different one each night,
as though an actor dressed in costume.

One day she came to the day she left Poland.
Her father was away on business.
She did not understand why soldiers came
or why there was such crying in the streets.
She packed her bag with dolls and underwear
so that the maid (they had maids!)
had to repack from the start.

That night with twenty other Jews
she huddled in the woods, waiting
to be smuggled across the border. She remembered

the muffled sound of pine needles and the smell
of resin sticking to her hands,
how her mother made a bed for them
from coats on the damp floor.
Then there came the sound of hoofs
and the voice of an officer in command.
She could see their lanterns from a distance
held like small moons in the low-lying branches.
Her mother held her mouth. She could hardly
breathe, and then she remembered being lifted,
lifted into the pines and set with her doll
on a branch by her brother, and then
the dark shape of her mother climbing like
a child into the tree, gathering about her
the thick skirt and fragile valise.
Beneath them a horse was stamping.
She saw the silver rings of the cavalry mount,
the steam blasting out of the stallion's nostrils.
She could see the dark curl of the soldier's moustache
so like her father's. Perhaps, she thought,
it is my father dressed in one of his costumes.
She wanted to call out to him, but her mother's
hand reasserted itself across her face.

They spent all night in the tree.
Monkeys, just like monkeys, she recalled,
and then a long walk to a farmhouse
where they were placed on the bottom of wagons.

To this day I awake
dreaming of the lantern smoking beneath me,
of wanting to call out to my father
sitting so handsome on his proud horse.

8

BLUEBERRY MAN

I was never the one to spot him walking
slowly up the street, pulling his yellow
wagon. It was always a brother or sister
who'd race home with the news. Then everything
spun into action like gulls at low tide.

Mother would shoo the children from the yard
and hide us out of danger in the living room,
warning with harsh whispers not to peek
from the windows and knowing we would anyway,
tracking the blueberry man across the porch
to where he knocked at the kitchen door.

Grandfather greeted him. Mother said
she was afraid. But I think she was jealous.
For though I was five or six, I knew I'd
never see such beautiful hair again. Hair
like a storybook princess. Great golden skeins,
falling halfway down his back. And such eyes,
freaked like a robin's egg and bobbing
beneath mascara waves of lashes. I remember
the Victory Red lips unfurling like a flag
when he spoke and the frilly shirt.

                               My brothers
giggled nervously. But I wasn't scared.
I wanted to pull the chiffon curtains back
and speak. But what would I say? That I knew
what it was to be alone? That I had heard
my own family scamper with trepidation
from my door when I was quarantined with
scarlet fever and no one but my mother was
allowed into my room?
                       I could have said:
I'm only a child but certain to end an outcast too.

Still, I said nothing, except once, a weak
goodby for which I was roundly scolded.
I used to ride my bike to his house, a tiny
cabin covered with angry brambles and
the hiss of intriguing bees, hoping we'd meet.
But he stayed inside during the day when he
wasn't peddling the wares he gathered at night.

One sleepless dawn I saw him coming home
with a kerosene lantern in one hand
and a silvery pail in the other.
Mother washed his berries twice to cleanse
them of his memory, as if he communicated
with his touch the fearful urge to dress
in women's clothing. For dessert she'd douse
the fruit with milk or pile them on peaks of
sour cream, chubby mountain climbers in the snow.
My brothers ate them greedily. But I
when everyone had left the table, would
still be seated, savoring the sweet juice
and the delicate flesh he had brought me.

THE LAYING ON OF HANDS

Each morning that spring, Sister Eve,
the local reader and advisor, watched
as I passed her storefront window on the way
to class in Hamilton Hall. Watched,
but never moved her head or eye except
inward, where framed in the glutinous mass
of her pupil, I hung like a bee in amber,
one shadow among the hundred forming
a pale cast over her yellow eye.

She sat alone beneath the neon hand
blazing with astrologic signs. At times
a daughter fixed tea from a samovar
or read from the back pages of the Bible.
And sometimes in the beaded hallway that
led to their quarters, her son would stand
naked above the waist but for a cross
carved in teak and slung on a leather band.

The door was opened in warm weather.
Incense rose with the sweet exhaust
of downtown buses on Amsterdam Avenue.
She called to me: "There's things you need to know,
for a dollar I'll tell you." "I'm late,"
I said. And she: "Don't be such a schoolboy.
Sit here with me. Gypsies don't bite."
And she flashed a row of broken teeth.
"Does it take long?" She shrugged
"It all depends upon the life, upon the hand."

Mine was full of incident. She squinted
at the fine print of my skin, a jeweler
bent over an uncut diamond and tracing
thin veins where the stone might break
clean and catch the purest light. "You will live,"

she decided at last, "in a house
by the water, a beautiful home filled
with books and rooms. I see no children
but as for love..." She stopped,
feeling the hand stiffen and sweat.

Then stooping lower, she nearly rested
the dark moon of her head in my arms.
"A young man's heart has secrets that an old
woman may not fathom. This line
rising up the index finger like a trail
of smoke remains a mystery even to me."
"Can no one tell," I asked. "Perhaps my son.
He shames his mother with his knowledge.
But he'll ask more to satisfy your curiosity."

I gave him what I had which wasn't much
for the lengthy fate he unrolled beneath
the frail light of his backroom.
He read my palm that morning, and then
the dim inscription nature leaves
on buttock and on thigh. He foretold
what was to come, and made it happen.
I do not ask that you believe in prophecy
who are so skeptical, so knowing and assured.
But if destinies are sealed at birth,
if the future can be read, then what better
place to read it than across our living flesh.

AUNT IDA'S LAST EVASION

Home for Christmas, I
visit my great aunt
Ida in the hospital.
I had grown that fall
a large scholarly beard
that stretched
like a dark smile
from ear to ear.
My mother goes in first
to set the stage, shakes
my aunt's arm grown thin
as a spider
in a web of tubing,
and whispers, "Look
who's here to see you!"
And turning to the door
my aunt screams, "MY GOD
IT'S THE ANGEL OF DEATH,"
but in Yiddish, "MEIN GOTT
MEIN GOTT," over and over
no matter how hard
we explain. A week later
she's dead. By her own orders,
attended by only clean
shaven men, a final ruse
to trick the demon
of the shtetl.
Foolish really, to think
he'd give up so easily
after coming all the way
to Worcester, Massachusetts
to get her. It takes
a dubbyk, how long?
maybe a week or two at most
to grow his whiskers back.

THE BALLAD OF AUNT ROSE

I dreamed I saw Aunt Rose alive
giving my room a sweep.
   "But, Rose," I said, "you're six years dead!"
Says she, "I couldn't sleep."
Says she, "I couldn't sleep."

"But all the pills you took," I said,
"was surely suicide."
   Says Rose, "I only took but one.
They call it cyanide,
they call it cyanide.

"A gun, of course, could do the trick
if pointed to my head,
   but guns are messy, don't you think,
and they'd stain the carpet red.
they'd stain the carpet red.

"Besides I wanted to be viewed
and dressed up to the hilt,
   and watch you pass in front of me
filled with Jewish guilt,
filled with Jewish guilt.

"For I took care of Sister Anne
inside the nursing home.
   Each night she asked me not to leave.
I pledged I'd never roam,
I pledged I'd never roam.

"And when she died at eighty-three
and was buried in her plot,
   the family took me out to eat.
That's all the thanks I got,
that's all the thanks I got.

"So you, young man, who think you're fit
and live a bachelor's life,
    just think of your two maiden aunts
and get yourself a wife,
and get yourself a wife.

" 'Cause when you're old and single, boy,
no one gives a pin.
    They dig a grave and say a prayer
and then they throw you in,
and then they throw you in."

I dreamed I saw Aunt Rose alive
giving my room a sweep.
    "But Rose," I said, "you're six years dead!"
Says she, "I couldn't sleep."
Says she, "I couldn't sleep."

CARDIOGRAM

It's not angina,
the pump too weak
to bail its foundering
ship, but a heart
that skips a beat
as it dances, trip-
ping over its own feet.
So says the specialist
I phone to ask
the status
of my father's condition,
and learn
the physician's
chief concern
is for candor.
"We feel your father
has pains of which
he never speaks
and fears
he won't express."
My job, I hear,
is to make him confess
the thousand injuries
he bore in silence.
"But it's too late,"
I want to say
and not a task
a son should bear.
For surely truth
cannot steady
his faltering heart.
Nor can we begin
to count each way
our love has failed him.

URBAN RENEWAL

Nothing is lost more completely than
the commonplaces of another
age. Sifting the phosphorescent loam,
archaeologists search the site where
Baltimore's first custom house once stood
for fragments which in this damp climate
resist the dark urge to decompose.

And years ago, not far away, I
saved the black Carrara glass façade
of the Anchor Bar & Restaurant,
the waterfront saloon where sailors
fought for the whores who lived upstairs
until the balls of the wrecking crew
laid everything flat for the highway.

One night Bob and Tom and I went out,
and we pried the slick sheets off the wall.
We placed the heavy panels, acid
etched with Deco letters, in a van,
then padded the sides to keep the panes
from shattering. By dawn Tom's mother
had her bare attic crammed to the eaves.

Later came accusations and lies,
the falling out of friends, the falling
in of prospects. I'm told our salvaged
front has disappeared from its hideout,
and next that Tom has died of causes
unexplained in another city,
his folks beyond our consolation.

Whatever we loosen from the past
burns in the solvent of memory.
Stalled at the choked throat of the harbor,
I wait in rush hour traffic, wait
where the Anchor Bar & Restaurant
had been, where tourists now browse boutiques
and the gulls wipe clean the glass-smooth sky.

SEDUCTION AT CAMDEN PASSAGE

This darting subcutaneous glance
is what passes on this island for a leer,
for of all the curious races

on this earth, the English are the least
flirtatious. That one brief look is all the hint
I'm likely to get. There'll be no more.

So I wander the flea market stalls,
beyond the sets of cracked Staffordshire and stands
of defoliated cloches to where

he sits feigning indifference, his eyes
averted, the cream of his Celtic skin browned
like a light custard done to a turn.

He's younger than I thought and shyer,
and he's pinned his ruthless curls like butterflies
fluttering hopelessly in the breeze.

Before him open three glass cases.
In one the beaky features of the Georges
snub the profiles of Antinous.

The next reveals clay pipes so dainty
they seem better suited for blowing bubbles
than consuming East Indian weed.

The last contains his prized possessions:
bits of hand-blown glass, an amber Roman bead,
a small brass buckle, Raleigh's perhaps,

Druid tools, a Jacobean chain,
the flotsam of ages no less profligate
than ours. "Where did you get such stuff?"

I ask, hoping he'll lift his head
to answer. "The coins I found in Islington
    along the banks of the old canal.

    It's easy enough with a metal
detector." "And these?" I ask, his head still down.
    He follows my fingers to a shard

    of glass earth has dyed the argentine
of a trout's underbelly. "For these," he said,
    "You keep your eyes firmly to the ground."

    At once I saw him pacing the fields
like Wordsworth's leech gatherer, doubled over
    and lonely as a cloud that has cast

    its nets to schools of enticing stars.
What miracles he must witness as he goes:
    the self-exhumation of the past,

    bodies rising of their own accord
from the absent-minded graves where the careless
    dead lost them or threw them away.

    His one duty is never to be
distracted, not by the kingfishers holding
    court at dawn by the river sallows,

    nor by the sun whose theatrical
exits and entrances are meant for stealing
    the show, and not by schoolboys riding

    in the backs of lorries, nor lorry
drivers, farmhands, cashiers and bank clerks, and not
    by any American tourists

who, having no past of their own,
can indulge in the untimeliness of sex
that leaves no trace and bears no issue.

Reproved, I thank him quickly, retreat
to the limits of the marketplace and catch
a final glimpse of his downcast face.

IN AND OUT OF THE GARDEN

Here there are no tourists, nor do
mechanical birds twitter as they choose
in the Tuileries, propelled by twisted
   rubber bands through the thick branches.

In other parts of the Jardin
du Luxembourg, auto-assemblers with
banners marked FIAT and AUDI may ogle
   and snooze, but in this trim corner

chairs are filled by the Parisians
who have álways filled them. Here all effort
is made to leave the order undisturbed,
   the state certain and unyielding,

despite the tendrilous effects
of heliotrope and wisteria.
At night the chairs are placed precisely back
   where sitters know they will find them,

and the gravel walkways are raked
into familiar grooves. Here the sloe-eyed
groundskeeper tiptoes across the slick grass
   to adjust the sprinklers, careful

that the water spills no farther
than the turf. He measures angles, the force
of fluids through the hose, prevailing winds,
   until he's certain not a drop

could cause a position to change
or alter an unalterable pose.
I am not asked to leave, but I can hear
   in the impatient rustling bush

this voice: *Rest if you like but don't
make yourself at home. These seats are taken,
the empty ones reserved. Your kind has its
places, but this isn't one of them.*

Out of a flower-bed rises
the bust of one who's kept his back to me,
who's given me the cold shoulder till now
when turning as I go, I catch

sight of his face, powerless and
ashamed, the features barely emerging
from the marble as if being dragged back
into his own viscosity —

like a swimmer who cannot break
the grip of waves that are carrying him
farther and still farther out to sea. Stamped
on the plinth, his name: Paul Verlaine.

EXCHANGES

The horror of spoiling is even
stronger than the anxiety of losing.
                    — Roland Barthes

"Care for *Le Monde?*" he asks, his arm
   outstretched with the journal. He speaks
in French, thinking I might be French
   and then in the delicately inflected Oxford
      of the educated Dutch, though he isn't
Dutch, but a Polynesian studying
history at the University. Why history?
   "Because we are the products of it,
and with biology it is the only fit subject,
      the rest but mere elaboration."

The express that morning is packed.
   We sit quite close, and his body,
more fragrance than flesh, drifts toward me
   with all its scent of unattended youth.
      I have seen him where? In a Gauguin
canvas? Standing above two bathing women,
the mask of a sea-beast in his hand?
   I ask him about Liège to which
we're heading, and before we reach our
   destination, he has offered to be my guide.

And what a tour!
   Approved more likely by the Chamber
of Horrors than the local Board of Trade.
   No cathedrals, museums, or bazaars.
      I'm taken to a suburb buried
behind the municipal gasworks where
children flap about like scraps
   of windblown paper, and the houses lean

24

tipsily together for comfort and support.
    We eat together in a bistro crowded as a hen-house

noisy with clattering dishes and the cluck
    of oriental tongues, the air
thick with fish and the gummy sweetness
    of overcooked rice. He tells me
        his plans for rescuing his people
    and to propitiate their fierce volcanic god
who spewed them out across the globe
    like Ten Lost Tribes. At first he speaks
        freely, but soon the passion makes him sullen,

or, at least, silent, as silent as he'll grow
    in my hotel room as I hold him
not against his wishes, but to his word.
    He swam that night against the sheets
        with long stiff strokes, a shipwreck
    survivor pulled to shore or a prodigal salmon
bound for home. When he tells me,
    "I've never done this before," I'm not
surprised. For who but a virgin loves
    with such ecstatic awkwardness or is
        the morning after so anxious to be seen again.

The very next evening I go to his room,
    the topmost rung of a medieval tower
that fortifies the citadel of learning.
    Swans, mute and vicious, patrol
        the moat, and I climb the stairs
till I hear from beneath his door a Mozart
    serenade rising higher than my foot
can mount. From his window I see rich
        shaded areas of varnished farmland

that trap the light and will not let it go.
    He stands behind me, captor and captivating,

kissing my neck here and here and here
    until the whole earth goes black.
        Back in New York, I write him regularly
    and he no less a correspondent
threatens often with a visit. Once he asked
    if I'd find him a job. But he never came.
Instead he left school and fell in with
        the dark side of the demimonde.

Then one night a call, collect. He needs
    money. He says a friend's in jail, held
by officials demanding bribes for his release.
    I don't believe a word of it.
        I can hear in his voice other voices
    saying: Take advantage of this rich
American. Get what you can while you have him.
    Exploit as you have been exploited.
I wired what he asked for but never wrote
        again, nor has he written me.

I have a reason for telling you this story.
    You want money? Take it. Take
all of it. What is love, if not a free
    exchange on a fairly open market
        by which we find our depreciated value.
    But be sure, my dear, to leave something
in return. A kiss, perhaps. A number
    where you can be reached. An article of clothing,
the sound of returning footsteps, or the fumble
        of keys before the door.

LANDSCAPE WITH CIRCE AND HER LOVERS

Modesty may be the last attribute
a witch would likely possess, but there hangs
a quattrocento Circe demurely
hiding her breasts with her hand, a painted
drapery tucked about her loins, leaving
one plump leg extending out to our view,
her sole arched like the heron's neck at left.

Surely no temptress even to sailors
so long at sea as Ulysses' crew, who
by then had found other recreation
to wile away their journey going nowhere.
Her sidelong, langorous, inattentive
look settles on the water, not caring
to survey her own demesne stretched about.

She holds a list of those she has transformed,
not all to swine, for she is circled by
a whole menagerie: birds and lizards,
bodies hoofed and scaled. Beneath the furred
and feathered faces float human eyes.
The screech owl wears a patient wisdom
and the falcon, the hunter's clear-eyed gaze.

And at the frame's still center, nearly hart
in hand, there beams the fawning countenance
of a stag. Like a schoolgirl unashamed
by her colt's caress, this Circe's at ease
only with such animal affection
as the nightingale's passionate lament
or the greyhound's unrequited kisses.

Rather than unlocking the beast in her
paramours, she cultivates their native
civility, as if their manly forms

had been throughout their lives the obstacle
to human fulfillment. "Be leopard, be
snake," she prompts without insistence, "Be
anything but the sailors that you are,

and I will love you." At once the light glows
dim and golden. A cottage in silhouette
peaks through the foliage, her home, no doubt.
Soon she will stir herself to milk the cows
and feed the chickens. What man could resist
such sweet imprisonment, or hope for more
release in the presence of a woman?

FENWAY COURT

No matter that rent-a-cops take the place
of liveried servants at her door, or that we
must present money, not calling cards, to gain

admission. Who did not spend an afternoon
at Mrs. Gardner's and fail to pay for it
afterward? We take her hand no less gracious

for being ghostly and begin the choir
of appreciative murmurs over this bronze
or that majolica or some rare arras

behind which who knows what intrigues were conceived;
all presented with the seeming careless
air of one with few important things to mind.

Take this fragment of Ulysses as he creeps
into camp, placed by the mistress's own hand
to remain forever at the landing's top.

At the foot of the stairs, we make out only
that one leg is gone, lost in the antique wars,
his dagger broken and his profile chipped.

But not until we rise to where the staircase
turns do we first face the fact (though there it's been
all along) that beneath his coat Ulysses

wears nothing except his masculinity,
the only endowment left by time intact,
with not even a circumcision to blunt

our recognition that his rockhard member
has been given life by the sculptor's hand, blood
flowing through the accidental veins of quartz.

29

A minor piece. Yet just the sort of gesture
to stop our mouths with its excess and force us,
were we critics, to swallow our mealy words.

What joy is found in such strokes of good fortune,
that here was a niche ready to receive him,
that this is a place where nothing less would do.

ROOKWOOD

Happiness, my dear, is not out of the question,
    but I had other aims in mind .
        when I asked if you might live with us;
for what passes as happiness may be found
      as easily on your father's farm
in avatars no rarer than the hired hand
blessed with the usual graces of his breed.
    Happiness is common: anyone willing
        to accept what he is given
may have it for the keeping. What I hold out
      is the power to say *No*,
no to the farmhands and the hucksters,
no to the miller and the milliner. No even to me.

    For someday — if I have done my work well —
        you shall toss me aside,
exhausting all the good I could have offered.
      Protest if you like.
I'm flattered you think me indispensable.
Still, if you're worth my effort, and you are,
      you shall surpass the little I have learned.
      A teacher is a Moses,
    who having struck his stone
too fiercely in the search for water, denies
      himself the vision of the Jordan's
        furthest bank and is left
    to witness others as they ford
the swiftness that blocks his own advancement.

    Cincinnati will not hold you
      as it has held me.
But for a girl who's never tasted more of society
      than fits in a box
    social, it will do better than
Boston, New York, or Philadelphia. Your uncle and I

will make sure you attend the better
　　　balls, concerts, and exhibitions.

Why just last week, Mr. Oscar Wilde was here
　　　giving a lecture. I see
　　the name means something to you.
You've read about him, no doubt, in *Leslie's*
　　Illustrated or *Harper's Weekly.*
　　　But what they say is lies,
lies as far as I could see. For journalists confuse
　　　a person's mettle with the iron
　　dug out of the earth, where to be pure
is weakness, refined fragility; strength achieved
　　alone by alloy with the baser elements.
　　　The Mr. Wilde I saw
was strong and elastic like the sunflower
　　　he is said to wear like
　　a coat-of-arms slung from his buttonhole.
I saw him quite close, even exchanged a word
　　or two as we walked through Rookwood
　　　Pottery, guests of Mrs. Nichols.

And there's a woman you must meet. A banker's wife.
　　　One day her work will gain the world's acclaim.
　　　Kings will demand
　　the vases and dinner plates she throws before us
　　　on the slopes of Mt. Adams.
　　　Royalty will feed on what she serves them,
form their tastes on our sense of beauty and delight.
　　It will take time. But as Mr. Wilde says,
　　　her work already shows
what a person may do if he chooses. And why not
　　　in America? For a potter
　　must have a feel for earth and fire,
and who better has than we, who having found
　　the ground untouched, know what it
　　　has always been? Our cities

are built on blazes. Our men are Shadrachs
at work in the fiery furnace.

See that vase there, the one with apple
blossoms ready to fall like a handkerchief
out of an old lady's palsied grip.
Ah, you like it, do you?
It's the work of Mr. Bailey. I like it too.
And when I first saw Mr. Wilde
dressed in a suit the shade of calla-lily leaves,
a shrimp pink necktie washed up upon his throat,
he was holding this vase. But he
did not like it. "Too branchy,"
he said. "Too branchy." And when Mr. Bailey began
to take offense, Mrs. Nichols
stopped him. "We are hardened to forests,"
she said, "and could never find a work 'too branchy.'
Yet this is just what we must learn." I bought
this vase, dear niece, to keep in front of me
in hope one day of finding it
"too branchy." But the forest and the trees are one
to me, as they are to you right now.
But you have the chance to learn the difference,
to recognize when the appetite is glutted
and stop before it sickens and dies.

Go see who's at the door.
It should be the young men I invited for tea:
Lionel Morrison, who leaves for Princeton
in the fall; and the surgeon's son,
a Matthew Barby, known around town
for his fine tenor voice. No blushing. Put down
the vase. Straighten your sash. We must
look our best for them.

ECLOGUE

The whores are afraid to cross the street
   unattended through the swirling cars.
Still no one offers to escort them
   and so like schoolgirls
wading daintily in a brook, they hold
   each other's hands and higher raise their skirts
to cool themselves in the stream of traffic.
   O Virgins, who among you is so innocent
or pure that she could run as they did
   splashing about in the blue exhaust?

RUBENESQUE

The fat woman wishes she were fatter.
"I am too small," she complains,
half-convinced of her insignificance
and yet unresigned to it.
She keeps to her room.
There she dominates, bending
the chairs to her iron will,
dragging the bed down with her
insatiable demands.
And because like Nature
she, too, abhors a vacuum,
all remaining space is filled
with memorabilia and underwear.
At night she prays,
"Please, Lord, make me so big
that when I move the tides will follow."

THE MINIATURIST

"I find beauty in things
that are small, fragile,
even microscopic. Here,"
she whispered, breathing in
the dust from off a tiny fern,
"smell the aroma. I could brew
tea from it, a mild subtle blend
were the plant not so small
or so slow in growing."
When she went to the beach
she would pick up only fragments
of shells, pieces worn thin
by the waves or faded by the sun.
"I couldn't think of taking
anything that was whole." And indeed
her house was a refuge for all
that was crippled and sick:
lame dogs, blind cats, fractured birds
who had to be fed by eyedropper.
Even the men in her life
had something broken about them.
Her former husband, a slight
good-looking delicate youth
(who proved himself impotent
to half of the neighborhood women)
often was viewed curled up
by her door like a wounded deer
waiting for her return. Once
he had tried to beat her.
And though she gave no resistance,
he wore a cast for months.

The Dancer Denies a Suitor

I don't suppose you tell the novelist,
"Oh what a lovely typewriter,
no wonder you're famous"?
And yet you look at my body and think,
"This is what it means to dance."

But I know you've neither watched me
dance nor looked at my body.
For if you had, you would have seen
that my art's the moment I just have left
and in the one I'm readying to enter,
reflections chased in a revolving door.

And my body. Well, look: a spine
too stiff, too broad, too muscled;
arms as soft as andirons; the steely legs
of harbor pilings. Were I put on the street,
no man would pay for me, or look
except to howl. A dancer is built
like a spinster—spare, tidy, and dry.

But then, we are made to disappear,
to leave only a trace of our presence.
I've dreamt of leaping up like spray
off the receding tide, to vaporize
in the shriveling sun and never return
to the sea's rhythm. Or fly legless like
a bird of Paradise, too proud to perch
on crusty boughs or in colorless streams.

I dreamt that I made an arabesque
balanced so perfectly I became suspended
in the position, unable to break the equipoise,
though the music played on and my partner

shook me. Even with the theater cleared,
I still stood locked from time and motion.

Sir, you desire just what you should hate
and claim as beautiful what's beauty's enemy.
Here, take my shadow—it's really what you want.
Or better yet, make love to the light.

No Knowledge but as Recollection

No, he wasn't always calm.
He was also capable of violent demonstrations.
I remember one day when Alcibiades
found himself alone with him,
a beautiful boy but crazy in love.
Socrates was asking his usual questions
on geometry and the afterlife,
but with the sun and that quiet manner,
Alcibiades forgot himself completely
and made a pass.
Socrates, outraged by this inattention,
lunged for his throat, crying,
"Now at least you'll recall what it was to die."
There was a terrible scene.
The same thing happened to Meno
and they were in the middle of the street.

OLD MAN SITTING IN A SHOPPING MALL

When I was young I gave my love
to what I thought was permanent:
God, Beauty or Eternal Truth.
But now the things that pass take hold
of my affections, and I'm lost
in you, my dear, who even now
are turning into someone else.

THE MADAME CONSIDERS HER FUTURE STATE

She'd prefer a life without memory,
one where nothing could tug her
from the pleasures of the moment
or place sensation in such perspective
that she'd feel her age.

How much better life could be
if days bore no resemblance to each other
and refused to spark those strings of association
which burst and fizzle like firecrackers
without altering the dark.

"One day I shall take the first
stiff steps to my window and see not the street
or the awnings of the shops below,
but rather a river and a little ribbon
of mist tied to the tresses of the pines...

and then it will not matter if I'm old
and have lost my innocence, since nothing
could give rise to the faces of my past.
Everything will have changed so utterly
with what would I have to compare them?"

In her small boudoir she began to construct
a chaos so complete no one could imagine
what might next appear.
Among her bed-clothes, newborn child
and ancient sage stood on equal footing.

This is like Heaven, she thought,
where angels never tire of singing praises.
For faced with an infinite deity
they neither repeat themselves
nor worry about order.

DOLDRUMS

Where in the theater of nature
did they find a winter like this?
With no beginning or end
it hardly qualifies for tragedy,

more like some medieval French romance
in a bad translation
limping from incident to incident
with all the characters disguised
and looking exactly alike.

And yet years from now
we'll recognize this winter
as the uneventful onset of a fatal disease.
We'll mark from this moment
the way things changed and froze.

"It was then," we'll recall,
"that the seasons began repeating themselves
like the lady announcing time over the telephone,
when we lost our faith in God
for strictly aesthetic reasons
and the sun became shiny and bright
like a trout in a crate of ice."

INTERCEPTED COURIER

In the end, the responsibility for cracking the code
falls on us, since we're assigned to breaking down the couriers.
And with the enemy better trained all the time, it's no easy task.
Though we keep up with the latest techniques
and constantly refine our methods,
it still boils down to a matter of time and patience.
The old ways prove the best.
The last one took fifteen days to crack
and even then it wasn't a complete confession,
just enough fragments to suggest a whole.

We began by stuffing him with drugs like a Christmas goose,
then flaying skin off his most sensitive parts.
We charged him with electrodes and burnt him with chemicals.
During the mild hallucinations, we told him his country had surrendered,
his leaders confessed,
or that we were his leaders and wished to honor him.
We alternately starved him and gorged him,
offered him women and men.
Twice his heart stopped. But we revived him
and told him he had died and led him through
a phantasmagoria of tortured souls and angelic choirs.
We told him we were god.
And though he bent down to kiss the hem
of our laboratory coats, he wouldn't confess.
Confess! we ordered. But then he thought we were the devil.
Damn the unpredictability of drugs!
At last we resorted to the oldest trick,
dressed one of our agents in drag and told the courier
we had his mother and were interrogating her in an adjacent room.
He begged to see her, but when brought to his side
she hurled the foulest curses at him.
"Why do you let them do this to me?" she screamed,
"You alone can make them stop."

With his last strength he crawled into her arms, sobbed for forgiveness
    and fell asleep.
We hadn't the heart to pull him away, besides we had what we wanted:
he let go in his babbling the last few clues needed to figure out the rest.
He died some hours later, an ancient, wrinkled man
who had been two weeks before so beautiful a specimen.
On him we focused our brutal need to know
which though the code is changed at the end of the month, is no less real.
Our men, on the average, last only a few days more.

ACTORS' EQUITY

I never could learn my lines.
I knew approximately what I was supposed to say,
but I was never letter-perfect.
Each time the curtain rose,
it was on a different play.
And the others, not knowing whether I'd
give them their cues, were forced to listen.
At first there was consternation.
But they were more involved when they listened
and there was excitement in the air.
They performed better, not knowing what to expect,
and gained a more intimate knowledge of their characters.
They praised me.
I had saved a dull and hollow play
from mechanical and thoughtless reproduction.
They had learned from each performance.
They admired my technique, my freshness, my flexibility,
and regretted replacing me in the middle of the run.
They wished me luck in finding another job.
The director told me he had a friend who taught mime
and insisted on writing his name
on the back of an envelope.
He wouldn't let me thank him.
"Don't say a word," he implored,
"It's enough if I can help."

THE ARTIST IS NO PHYSICIAN

"The figure should be natural and relaxed,"
    asserted Mucha to his drawing class,
but didn't tell that he bent the Job girl's fingers
    back into a knuckle-breaking arabesque
and thereby crossed her smile with a wince,
    or how his son complained of feeling deformed
    after sitting for his father. The truth is
that beauty pursued from a single angle
    has never added to a person's comfort.

THE DEDICANT

for Gordon Lester-Massman

Dear Melville,
       How should I receive this gesture,
my name carved on your latest craft, a gilded
figurehead condemned to bite the spume or drown
in waves of applause? Some dedicate their works
to flatter, some to repay artistic debts.
But this act I take as challenge and as curse.
Far safer always to wear my scarlet A
than to face the blank indifference of your beast.

Whatever white may mean to others, for me
it signifies the unmarked page I dare not
write, the signs and portents I left unnoted,
unexcised. This unmounted Leviathan
reminds me that I must watch my every word,
being too well understood each time I speak
and no master yet of your amphibian
ambiguity. What would I give to write
with such impunity your damnable truth,
to wail heresy before the city gate!
I tried anonymity. They found me out.
I lived in isolation. They came on foot
and phaeton, knocking politely at my door.
O Melville, may you gain with this book a long
deserved obscurity, leaving you but bees
and locusts to convert in the wilderness.
There I will join you, once shorn of well-wishers,
abolitionists, in-laws, office-seekers,
bluestockings with bulldog faces, reformers,
and the bubbling raptures of Christian women.

Did I ever tell you that once I, too, searched
waters for what would rise up white and deadly?

I come from a sailing family, and I
am a skilled oarsman. Given a pond, paddle
and a boat, I'm as fleet as a dragonfly
and as nimble as a minnow. Our home then
was Concord. Sophia and I were in bed
when we heard a rap at the door, a neighbor
come to tell us Martha Hunt, a country girl,
had thrown herself in the river. She'd been seen
shuffling along its banks all day distracted,
though no one in this high-minded town lowered
himself to offer comfort. The week before,
her sister, fearful of some dreadful act,
found her at the water's edge and brought her home.

We all knew Martha Hunt, a kind-hearted child,
who left the well-managed farm of her father
for Emerson's Promised Land. She wore brand new
overshoes to go and meet the oversoul,
then learned too late it's better to be bootless.
At home she lived an unconscious life, her fixed
routine driving off the pains of existence.
After twenty years of milking cows at dawn
one hardly feels a thing. But there at Concord,
faced daily with religious questions, our wounds
mount up, lacerations ooze, superficial abrasions
score deep as ruts in springtime roads; in short,
she sickened from too much talk of ecstasy.
At dusk they found her bonnet beached, her hanky
drifting. The search party could not risk to wait
for morning. They called to press *The Pond Lily*,
my rowboat, into immediate service.

It was summer, Melville, but the air was raw.
The weeds smelled rank, and the stars leered from the sky.
On shore, lanterns sizzled a rheumy ocher
and the one we kept on board refused to flinch,
but held a steady clinical detachment.
It was nearly dawn when I found her, lodged down
in a marsh where she ran aground. It took two

of us to bring her body to the surface
because it had grown by then stiff and swollen.
She was white, as white as your whale, in a white
summer dress. Her arms were outstretched, her mouth curled
in a devil's grin, and her hair was eel grass.
We let none of the women see her. We kept
her coffin closed even to her family.
You should have seen her father, the old farmer.
He did not cry or speak. He only appeared
anxious to get back to his plowing, as if
his daughter had been just one more crop that failed.

I have been long at this, but I have not yet
said what I should have admitted long ago:
I understand quite well what you want of me.
I am not ignorant of what men can mean
to each other. Sophia's gift of the head
of Antinous hangs right in my study.
For her it is a sign of ideal friendship,
but I know it is something more. O Melville,
I'm not fit to entertain the void like you.
I can't bear the barrenness of pure desire.
Love, for me, must be linked to the intercourse
of family: carriages, muffs, firescreens,
all the bric-a-brac of domesticity,
or else like Martha Hunt I shall be wailing
by the side of the choked, unmoving river.

If you visit, I will see you meet my friend,
Thoreau. He's an odd-looking man, I admit,
but his soul doesn't shrink from isolation.
In Concord, he used to visit for hours
and talk. He's a friend whom I have also failed.

Affectionately yours,
                    Nathaniel Hawthorne